PALERMO

TRAVEL GUIDE 2024

Discover Palermo: Your Ultimate Travel Companion for Unforgettable Adventures, Itineraries, Hidden Gems, Things to do, and Local Delights in Sicily's Vibrant Capital.

Lydia A. Eyler

TABLE OF CONTENTS

INTRODUCTION
DISCOVERING PALERMO: A
JOURNEY OF WONDER AND
ENCHANTMENT

Palermo, the radiant jewel of Sicily, holds within its embrace a world of wonder and enchantment. My journey through its winding streets and ancient alleys was a revelation, a tapestry woven with threads of history, culture, and culinary delights.

Arriving in Palermo felt like stepping into a living museum, where each cobblestone street whispered tales of times long past. The city's architectural marvels, from the majestic Palermo Cathedral to the resplendent Norman Palace and Palatine Chapel, stood as silent witnesses to centuries of history and tradition. The grandeur of Teatro Massimo, with its opulent interiors and spellbinding performances, left me breathless, while the somber beauty of the Capuchin Catacombs offered a haunting glimpse into Palermo's complex past.

Yet, it was not just the city's landmarks that captured my

heart; it was the vibrant tapestry of life that unfolded around every corner. The lively chaos of Ballarò Market, where vendors peddle their wares amidst a symphony of sights, sounds, and smells, filled me with a sense of exhilaration and wonder. Exploring Palermo's street art scene was like embarking on a visual odyssey, each mural a testament to the city's creativity and spirit.

Venturing beyond the city limits, I discovered a land of breathtaking beauty and natural wonders.

Whether basking in the sun on the golden sands of Mondello Beach or gazing in awe at the rugged majesty of Mount Etna, every moment spent exploring Sicily's landscapes was a revelation.

But it was the warmth and generosity of Palermo's people that truly left an indelible mark on my heart. From the jovial banter of market vendors to the genuine hospitality of strangers-turned-friends, I was welcomed into the fold with open arms and warm smiles.

In these pages, I invite you to embark on your own journey of discovery through Palermo. Whether you're planning your first visit or longing to relive the magic of past adventures, may this guide serve as your compass, guiding you through the myriad wonders that await in this timeless city. Welcome to Palermo, where every moment is a celebration of life, culture, and the endless possibilities of discovery.

Overview of Palermo's History and Culture

Palermo, the vibrant capital of Sicily, is a city steeped in a rich tapestry of history and culture. From its ancient origins as a Phoenician settlement to its modern-day status as a bustling metropolis, Palermo has been shaped by a diverse array of influences that have left an indelible mark on its character and identity.

Ancient Origins and Early Settlements

The history of Palermo dates back over 2,700 years, making it one of the oldest cities in Europe. It was originally founded by the Phoenicians in the 8th century BC, who established a thriving port settlement known as Ziz. The strategic location of Palermo, nestled between Europe and Africa, made it a coveted prize for numerous civilizations throughout history.

In the 5th century BC, Palermo came under Greek rule and was renamed Panormus, meaning "all-port," reflecting its importance as a maritime hub. Under Greek influence, the city flourished as a center of trade and culture, with the establishment of theaters, temples, and public buildings.

Roman Rule and Imperial Legacy

During the First Punic War in the 3rd century BC, Palermo fell under Roman control and became an integral part of the Roman Empire. Under Roman rule, the city experienced a period of expansion and prosperity, with the construction of aqueducts, baths, and amphitheaters.

Palermo's strategic location at the crossroads of Mediterranean trade routes made it a vital hub for commerce and communication. The Romans also left their mark on the city's culture and architecture, with influences that can still be seen today in its historic landmarks and archaeological sites.

Medieval Splendor and Arab Influence

In the 9th century AD, Palermo was conquered by the Arabs, who brought with them a rich cultural heritage that would profoundly shape the city's identity. Under Arab rule, Palermo experienced a golden age of prosperity and enlightenment, known as the Arab-Norman period.

During this time, Palermo became a center of learning and scholarship, attracting scholars, poets, and philosophers from across the Islamic world. The Arabs also introduced innovations in agriculture, irrigation, and architecture, leaving behind a legacy of stunning mosques, palaces, and gardens.

Norman Conquest and Renaissance Revival

In the 11th century, Palermo was conquered by the Normans, who integrated Arab, Byzantine, and Western influences to create a unique cultural synthesis. Under Norman rule, the city experienced a period of artistic and architectural revival, with the construction of magnificent churches, cathedrals, and palaces.

The Norman kings of Sicily, such as Roger II and Frederick II, were patrons of the arts and sciences, fostering a climate of creativity and innovation. Palermo's cathedral, with its blend of Norman, Arab, and Byzantine elements, stands as a testament to this cultural fusion.

Spanish Dominion and Baroque Splendor

In the 16th century, Palermo came under Spanish rule and experienced a period of economic decline and social unrest. However, this era also saw the emergence of the Baroque style in architecture and art, with the construction of ornate churches, palaces, and fountains.

The Spanish influence can still be seen in Palermo's historic neighborhoods, with their winding streets, colorful facades, and lively piazzas. The city's Baroque masterpieces, such as the Quattro Canti and the Church of San Cataldo, reflect the grandeur and opulence of this period.

Modern Era and Cultural Renaissance

In the 19th century, Palermo witnessed a resurgence of cultural and artistic activity, fueled by the Romantic movement and the rise of nationalism. The city became a center of political activism and intellectual debate, with the emergence of literary figures such as Giuseppe Tomasi di Lampedusa and Leonardo Sciascia.

Despite periods of political turmoil and social upheaval, Palermo has continued to thrive as a vibrant cultural capital, attracting artists, writers, and musicians from around the world. Today, the city's rich cultural heritage is celebrated through its museums, galleries, festivals, and culinary traditions, ensuring that the legacy of Palermo's history lives on for future generations to discover and cherish.

Why Palermo Should be Your Next Travel Destination

Palermo, the vibrant capital of Sicily, beckons travelers with its irresistible blend of history, culture, and culinary delights. As someone who has had the pleasure of exploring this enchanting city firsthand, I can attest to the myriad reasons why Palermo should be at the top of your travel itinerary.

1. Rich History and Cultural Heritage

Palermo boasts a history that spans over 2,700 years, making it one of the oldest cities in Europe. From its ancient origins as a Phoenician settlement to its medieval splendor under Arab and Norman rule, the city is a living testament to the diverse civilizations that have shaped its identity.

Walking through Palermo's historic streets is like stepping back in time, with each corner revealing a new chapter in the city's storied past. From the awe-inspiring architecture of its cathedrals and palaces to the vibrant street life of its markets and piazzas, every moment spent exploring Palermo is a journey through history.

2. Architectural Marvels and Landmarks

Palermo is home to a wealth of architectural treasures that are sure to captivate visitors of all interests. The city's iconic landmarks, such as the Palermo Cathedral, Norman Palace, and Teatro Massimo, showcase a fascinating blend of styles from across the centuries.

During my own visit to Palermo, I was struck by the sheer grandeur of these architectural marvels. Standing beneath the soaring dome of the Palermo Cathedral or gazing up at the ornate mosaics of the Palatine Chapel, I couldn't help but marvel at the craftsmanship and artistry that went into creating these masterpieces.

3. Vibrant Street Life and Cultural Scene

One of the highlights of any visit to Palermo is immersing yourself in the city's vibrant street life and cultural scene. From the bustling markets of Ballarò and Vucciria to the lively festivals and events that take place throughout the year, there's never a dull moment in Palermo.

During my time in Palermo, I spent countless hours wandering through the city's markets, sampling fresh produce, and soaking up the sights and sounds of daily life. Whether I was savoring a cannolo from a street vendor or admiring the colorful street art that adorns the city's walls, I was constantly reminded of the rich tapestry of culture and tradition that defines Palermo.

4. Culinary Delights and Gastronomic Adventures

No visit to Palermo would be complete without indulging in the city's world-renowned culinary delights. From savory street food to gourmet dining experiences, Palermo offers a tantalizing array of flavors and dishes to satisfy even the most discerning palate.

One of my most memorable experiences in Palermo was taking a street food tour, where I had the opportunity to sample arancini, panelle, and other Sicilian specialties from local vendors. Each bite was a revelation, bursting with flavor and history, and left me craving more long after the tour had ended.

5. Warm Hospitality and Authentic Experiences

Last but certainly not least, what truly sets Palermo apart is the warmth and hospitality of its people. From the moment I arrived, I was welcomed with open arms and made to feel like part of the family. Whether I was chatting with locals at a cafe or sharing a meal with newfound friends, the genuine warmth and generosity of the people of Palermo left a lasting impression on me.

Palermo offers a travel experience like no other, with its rich history, architectural marvels, vibrant culture, and delicious cuisine. Whether you're a history buff, a foodie, or simply someone looking for an unforgettable adventure, Palermo has something to offer everyone. So why wait? Start planning your trip to Palermo today and discover the magic of this enchanting city for yourself.

Best Time to Visit Palermo and Major Events

Palermo, with its rich history, vibrant culture, and stunning landscapes, offers something special to visitors throughout the year. However, choosing the best time to visit depends on your preferences, interests, and tolerance for crowds. Understanding the major events and festivals in Palermo can help you plan your trip to coincide with the experiences that matter most to you.

Spring (March to May)

Springtime in Palermo is a delightful season characterized by mild temperatures, blooming flowers, and a sense of renewal. It's an ideal time to explore the city's historic sites, enjoy outdoor activities, and immerse yourself in Sicilian culture.

Weather: During spring, temperatures in Palermo range from 15°C to 25°C (59°F to 77°F), providing comfortable conditions for sightseeing, hiking, and exploring the city's gardens and parks.

Major Events and Festivals:

Easter: Easter is a significant religious holiday in Palermo, marked by processions, religious services, and traditional celebrations. The city comes alive with vibrant displays of faith and devotion, making it a fascinating time to experience Sicilian culture.

Feast of Saint Rosalia: Celebrated on May 15th, the Feast of Saint Rosalia is one of Palermo's most important festivals, honoring the city's patron saint. Festivities include processions, concerts, fireworks, and street fairs, attracting locals and visitors alike.

Tourist Crowds: While spring sees fewer tourists compared to the peak summer season, popular attractions may still have moderate crowds, especially during Easter and other major events. Planning ahead and booking accommodations and tours in advance can help you avoid long lines and ensure a more enjoyable experience.

Summer (June to August)

Summer is the peak tourist season in Palermo, thanks to its warm weather, long days, and lively atmosphere. It's the perfect time to soak up the sun on the city's beaches, indulge in Sicilian cuisine, and attend outdoor events and festivals.

Weather: Summer temperatures in Palermo soar, with highs averaging around 30°C to 35°C (86°F to 95°F). The city enjoys plenty of sunshine, making it ideal for beachgoers and outdoor enthusiasts.

Major Events and Festivals:

Palermo Pride: Held in June, Palermo Pride is a colorful celebration of diversity and LGBTQ+ rights, featuring parades, parties, and cultural events throughout the city.

Festa di Santa Rosalia: In July, Palermo pays homage to its patron saint with the Festa di Santa Rosalia. Highlights include religious processions, concerts, and street performances, culminating in a spectacular fireworks display.

Tourist Crowds: Summer attracts the highest number of tourists to Palermo, particularly in July and August. Popular attractions and beaches can be crowded, so it's advisable to arrive early or visit during off-peak hours to avoid the crowds.

Autumn (September to November)

Autumn offers a more tranquil and temperate experience in Palermo, with pleasant weather, fewer tourists, and the opportunity to enjoy cultural events and harvest festivals.

Weather: Temperatures in autumn range from 20°C to 25°C (68°F to 77°F), making it an ideal time for outdoor activities such as hiking, wine tasting, and exploring the countryside.

Major Events and Festivals:

Festival di Morgana: Held in September, the Festival di Morgana celebrates the folklore and traditions of Sicily with music, dance, and theatrical performances.

Palermo International Film Festival: In November, film enthusiasts gather in Palermo to enjoy screenings of international and independent films, as well as workshops, panels, and networking events.

Tourist Crowds: Autumn sees fewer tourists compared to summer, making it an excellent time to visit if you prefer a quieter and more relaxed atmosphere. However, popular attractions may still have moderate crowds, especially during weekends and special events.

Winter (December to February)

Winter in Palermo is mild and relatively quiet, offering a unique opportunity to explore the city's cultural attractions, indulge in seasonal cuisine, and experience Sicilian Christmas traditions.

Weather: Winter temperatures in Palermo range from 10°C to 15°C (50°F to 59°F), with occasional rain showers. While cooler than other seasons, the weather is still mild enough to enjoy outdoor activities and sightseeing.

Major Events and Festivals:

Christmas Markets: Throughout December, Palermo's streets come alive with festive decorations, Christmas markets, and holiday events. Visitors can shop for gifts, sample traditional sweets, and enjoy seasonal entertainment.

Capodanno (New Year's Eve): New Year's Eve in Palermo is celebrated with fireworks, parties, and live music in the city's piazzas and nightclubs. It's a lively and festive atmosphere, with locals and visitors ringing in the new year together.

Tourist Crowds: Winter is the quietest time of year in Palermo, with fewer tourists and shorter lines at popular attractions. It's an excellent time to visit if you prefer a more authentic and intimate experience of the city.

Each season offers its own unique charms and attractions in Palermo, making it a destination worth visiting year-round. Whether you're drawn to the vibrant festivals of summer, the tranquil beauty of autumn, or the festive atmosphere of winter, there's something for everyone to enjoy in this captivating city. By considering your preferences and interests, you can choose the best time to visit Palermo and create memories that will last a lifetime.

CHAPTER 1:
GETTING TO KNOW PALERMO

Getting to know Palermo is like unraveling a tapestry of history, culture, and culinary delights. Set against the backdrop of the stunning Sicilian landscape, this vibrant city offers a captivating blend of ancient landmarks, bustling markets, and lively street life. Whether you're exploring its historic streets on foot, sampling local delicacies at a traditional trattoria, or soaking up the Mediterranean sun on its picturesque beaches, Palermo beckons travelers with its irresistible charm and endless possibilities for discovery.

Geographic Location and Climate

Palermo, the bustling capital of Sicily, is situated on the northern coast of the island, overlooking the azure waters of the Tyrrhenian Sea. Its strategic location at the crossroads of Europe, Africa, and the Mediterranean has endowed it with a rich history and vibrant cultural heritage.

The city's geographic coordinates are approximately 38.1157° N latitude and 13.3615° E longitude. Nestled between the rugged peaks of the Sicilian mountains to the south and the shimmering coastline to the north, Palermo enjoys a stunning natural setting that has captivated travelers for centuries.

The weather in Palermo is Mediterranean, with hot, dry summers and warm, rainy winters. Average temperatures range from around 30°C (86°F) in the summer months to 10°C (50°F) in the winter, making it an ideal destination for travelers seeking warm weather year-round.

Summer is the peak tourist season in Palermo, with visitors flocking to its beaches, historic sites, and cultural events. However, for those looking to avoid the crowds and enjoy more temperate weather, spring and fall are also excellent times to visit.

Transportation Options: Getting In and Around the City

Getting to Palermo

Palermo is easily accessible by air, sea, and land, making it a convenient destination for travelers from around the world.

By Air: The city is served by Falcone-Borsellino Airport (PMO), located approximately 35 kilometers west of the city center. Falcone-Borsellino Airport is a major hub for domestic and international flights, with regular connections to destinations across Europe, North Africa, and the Middle East. From the airport, visitors can reach the city center by taxi, bus, or shuttle service.

By Sea: Palermo is also a popular cruise ship destination, with numerous cruise lines offering Mediterranean itineraries that include stops in the city. The Port of Palermo is located just a short distance from the city center and is well-connected to the rest of Sicily and mainland Italy by ferry services.

By Land: Travelers can also reach Palermo by train, bus, or car. The city is served by several major highways, including the A19 and A29, which connect it to other cities and regions across Sicily. Additionally, Palermo's central train and bus stations offer regular services to destinations throughout the island and mainland Italy.

Getting Around Palermo

Once you've arrived in Palermo, getting around the city is easy thanks to its well-developed transportation network.

Public Transportation: Palermo has an extensive public transportation system that includes buses, trams, and a metro line. The city's buses are operated by AMAT and provide convenient access to key attractions, neighborhoods, and suburbs. Tickets can be purchased from kiosks, tabaccherie (tobacco shops), or on board the bus itself.

Walking and Cycling: Palermo's compact city center is best explored on foot or by bicycle. Many of the city's top attractions, including the Palermo Cathedral, Quattro Canti, and Ballarò Market, are within walking distance of each other, making it easy to navigate on foot. For those looking to explore further afield, bike rental services are available throughout the city.

Taxis and Ridesharing: Taxis are readily available in Palermo and can be hailed on the street or booked in advance by phone. Alternatively, ridesharing services such as Uber and Lyft also operate in the city, providing another convenient option for getting around.

Car Rental: While driving in Palermo's historic city center can be challenging due to narrow streets and limited parking, renting a car can be a convenient option for exploring the surrounding countryside and coastal areas. Numerous car rental companies have offices at Falcone-Borsellino Airport and throughout the city.

Palermo's convenient location, favorable climate, and excellent transportation options make it an ideal destination for travelers seeking to explore the beauty and charm of Sicily. Whether you're arriving by air, sea, or land, getting to and around Palermo is easy and hassle-free, allowing you to focus on enjoying all that this enchanting city has to offer.

Language, Communication, and Essential Phrases in Italian

Palermo, the vibrant capital of Sicily, welcomes visitors with open arms and a rich tapestry of language and culture. While Italian is the official language spoken in Palermo, you'll also encounter Sicilian dialect, which reflects the city's unique heritage and history. Whether you're ordering a cappuccino at a local cafe or asking for directions to a historic landmark, knowing a few basic phrases in Italian will enhance your experience and help you connect with the locals on a deeper level.

Greetings and Pleasantries:

"Ciao" - Hello / Hi (used informally)

"Buongiorno" - Good morning

"Buonasera" - Good evening

"Buona notte" - Good night

"Grazie" - Thank you

"Prego" - You're welcome

Common Expressions:

"Per favore" - Please

"Mi scusi" - Excuse me

"Mi dispiace" - I'm sorry

"Come stai?" - How are you? (informal)

"Mi chiamo..." - My name is...

"Non capisco" - I don't understand

Numbers and Directions:

"Uno, due, tre" - One, two, three

"Dove si trova...?" - Where is...?

"A sinistra" - To the left

"A destra" - To the right

"Diritto" - Straight ahead

When engaging with locals, remember to speak slowly and clearly, and don't be afraid to use gestures or simple drawings to help convey your message. Most Palermitani will appreciate your efforts to speak their language and will respond with warmth and hospitality.

Currency and Money Matters

Understanding the currency and money matters in Palermo is essential for a smooth and hassle-free travel experience. The official currency of Italy is the Euro (EUR), which is used throughout Palermo and the rest of Sicily. Here's what you need to know about currency exchange, payment methods, and budgeting during your visit:

Currency Exchange:

Currency exchange offices, known as "cambio," can be found in tourist areas, airports, and major transportation hubs in Palermo. They offer competitive exchange rates and convenient services for converting foreign currency into euros.

Banks and post offices also provide currency exchange services, although they may have limited hours of operation, especially on weekends and holidays.

ATMs (bancomat) are widely available throughout Palermo and accept major credit and debit cards, including Visa, Mastercard, and American Express. To prevent any problems with card transactions, make sure your bank is informed of your trip.

Paying for Goods and Services:

Cash is still widely used for everyday transactions in Palermo, especially at local markets, street vendors, and smaller establishments. It's recommended to carry a mix of cash and cards for convenience.

Credit and debit cards are accepted at most hotels, restaurants, shops, and attractions in Palermo. However, some smaller businesses may prefer cash payments, so it's always a good idea to ask before making a purchase.

Tipping is not obligatory in Italy, but it's customary to leave a small gratuity (around 10%) for excellent service at restaurants, cafes, and bars.

Budgeting and Expenses:

Palermo is generally an affordable destination compared to other major European cities, with reasonable prices for accommodation, dining, and transportation.

It's advisable to budget accordingly for sightseeing tours, entrance fees to attractions, souvenirs, and dining out to ensure that you make the most of your trip without overspending.

Keep in mind that prices may vary depending on the season, location, and type of establishment, so it's a good idea to research and plan ahead to avoid any surprises.

By familiarizing yourself with the currency and money matters in Palermo, you'll be well-prepared to manage your finances and enjoy a memorable and stress-free travel experience in this enchanting city.

Recommended Accommodation Options

Choosing the right accommodation is a crucial aspect of planning any trip to Palermo. The city offers a diverse range of lodging options, from charming boutique hotels to luxurious resorts and budget-friendly hostels. Your choice of accommodation can significantly impact your overall experience, so it's essential to consider factors such as location, amenities, and budget when making your decision.

1. Luxury Hotels

For travelers seeking the epitome of comfort, elegance, and impeccable service, Palermo boasts a selection of luxurious five-star hotels. These establishments often feature lavish rooms and suites, gourmet dining options, spa facilities, and stunning views of the city or the sea.

Grand Hotel Villa Igiea - MGallery: Nestled on the shores of the Gulf of Palermo, this historic hotel offers a perfect blend of old-world charm and modern luxury. Set within a magnificent Liberty-style building, guests can enjoy spacious rooms, lush gardens, and a breathtaking view of the sea. The hotel's sophisticated restaurant, Le Cupole, serves exquisite Sicilian cuisine.

Grand Hotel Piazza Borsa: Situated in the heart of the historic district, Grand Hotel Piazza Borsa combines opulence with convenience. The hotel is housed in a former convent and features elegantly decorated rooms, a rooftop terrace with panoramic views, and a spa where guests can unwind after a day of exploration.

2. Boutique Hotels

Palermo's historic neighborhoods are dotted with unique boutique hotels that offer personalized service and a distinctive ambiance. These smaller, independently-owned establishments provide an intimate and immersive experience, often reflecting the local culture and style.

Bio Hotel Palermo: Located near the vibrant Vucciria Market, Bio Hotel Palermo is a boutique eco-friendly hotel that emphasizes sustainability.

The hotel features bright and modern rooms, a rooftop terrace, and a commitment to environmentally friendly practices. Guests can enjoy locally sourced organic breakfast options.

BB 22 Charming Rooms & Apartments: Tucked away in a quiet street in the city center, BB 22 combines the warmth of a bed and breakfast with the style of a boutique hotel. The individually decorated rooms showcase a mix of contemporary design and Sicilian charm. Guests appreciate the personalized attention from the friendly staff.

3. Mid-Range Hotels

For those seeking a balance between comfort and affordability, Palermo offers a variety of mid-range hotels that provide excellent amenities and convenient locations.

Artemisia Palace Hotel: Situated near the Teatro Massimo, Artemisia Palace Hotel is a stylish mid-range option with comfortable rooms and a rooftop terrace offering panoramic views of the city. The hotel's central location makes it easy for guests to explore Palermo's historic sites and cultural attractions.

Hotel del Centro: Nestled in the heart of the historic district, Hotel del Centro offers straightforward comfort at a reasonable price. The hotel provides cozy rooms, a welcoming atmosphere, and a convenient location within walking distance of popular landmarks such as the Quattro Canti.

4. Budget Accommodations

Palermo caters to budget-conscious travelers with a variety of affordable accommodation options, including hostels, guesthouses, and budget hotels.

Hostel Agata: Perfect for backpackers and solo travelers, Hostel Agata provides budget-friendly accommodation in a lively neighborhood. The hostel offers dormitory-style rooms, communal spaces, and a friendly atmosphere. Its central location makes it easy for guests to explore Palermo on foot.

Casa Orioles: This guesthouse, located near the historic Ballarò Market, provides affordable rooms with a local touch. Casa Orioles offers clean and simple accommodations, allowing budget-conscious travelers to experience the authentic atmosphere of Palermo's markets and streets.

5. Vacation Rentals

For a more independent and home-like experience, vacation rentals are a popular option in Palermo. These include apartments, villas, and houses that allow visitors to live like locals and enjoy a more flexible and personalized stay.

AIRBNB: Palermo has a wide selection of Airbnb options, ranging from cozy apartments in the city center to charming villas in the outskirts. This allows travelers to choose accommodation that suits their preferences and enjoy the comfort of a home away from home.

Before making a reservation, it's advisable to consider your travel priorities and preferences. Whether you're seeking a luxury retreat, a charming boutique experience, or a budget-friendly stay, Palermo offers accommodation options to suit every taste and budget, enhancing your overall experience in this captivating Sicilian city.

CHAPTER 2:
EXPLORING PALERMO'S TOP ATTRACTIONS

Palermo, the vibrant capital of Sicily, is a treasure trove of historical and cultural wonders waiting to be discovered. From magnificent palaces to charming markets, there's something to captivate every traveler in this bustling city. Visit the majestic Palermo Cathedral, a masterpiece of Norman architecture, and stroll through the bustling streets of the historic Ballarò Market. Don't miss the iconic Palazzo dei Normanni, home to the stunning Palatine Chapel, adorned with breathtaking mosaics. With its rich history, eclectic architecture, and mouthwatering cuisine, Palermo promises an unforgettable exploration for all who visit.

Palermo Cathedral: Marvel at Sicily's Architectural Jewel

Palermo Cathedral, or Cattedrale di Palermo in Italian, stands as a testament to the city's rich history and cultural heritage. Located in the heart of Palermo's historic center, this magnificent cathedral is a must-visit attraction for anyone exploring the capital of Sicily.

History and Architecture:

Palermo Cathedral boasts a fascinating history that spans over nine centuries, reflecting the diverse influences of the civilizations that have shaped Sicily. The original structure was built in 1185 by Walter Ophamil, the Archbishop of Palermo, on the site of an earlier Byzantine basilica and an Arab mosque. Over the centuries, the cathedral underwent numerous renovations and expansions, resulting in its eclectic blend of architectural styles, including Norman, Gothic, Baroque, and Neoclassical elements.

One of the most striking features of Palermo Cathedral is its imposing façade, characterized by intricate carvings, ornate sculptures, and a majestic central portal adorned with biblical scenes and figures. The façade reflects the cathedral's evolution over time, with each section representing a different historical period and cultural influence.

Inside the cathedral, visitors can marvel at its soaring nave, elegant columns, and majestic domes adorned with stunning mosaics and frescoes. The highlight of the interior is the Royal Chapel, dedicated to Saint Rosalia, the patron saint of Palermo. The chapel features exquisite marble reliefs, a richly decorated ceiling, and the tombs of several Sicilian monarchs, including Roger II and Frederick II.

Must-See Attractions:

The Treasury: Located within the cathedral complex, the Treasury houses a remarkable collection of religious artifacts, including precious gold and silver objects, intricately embroidered vestments, and ancient manuscripts. Highlights include the Crown of Constance, an iconic symbol of Sicilian royalty, and the Reliquary of Saint Rosalia, believed to contain the saint's remains.

The Roof Terraces: For a unique perspective of Palermo Cathedral and panoramic views of the city, visitors can ascend to the roof terraces via a series of narrow staircases. From this vantage point, you can admire the cathedral's intricate architecture, as well as breathtaking vistas of Palermo's historic center, the surrounding mountains, and the azure waters of the Mediterranean Sea.

The Crypt: Beneath the cathedral lies the Crypt, a subterranean chamber that houses the tombs of Palermo's bishops and archbishops. The Crypt offers a fascinating glimpse into the city's religious history and provides a tranquil space for reflection and contemplation.

Visiting Tips:

Opening Hours: Palermo Cathedral is typically open to visitors daily, with varying opening hours for different sections of the cathedral. It's advisable to check the official website or inquire locally for the most up-to-date information on opening hours and guided tours.

Dress Code: As a place of worship, visitors are expected to dress modestly when entering Palermo Cathedral. Avoid wearing revealing clothing such as shorts, sleeveless tops, or mini-skirts, and consider bringing a shawl or scarf to cover bare shoulders or legs if needed.

Guided Tours: To gain a deeper understanding of the cathedral's history, architecture, and significance, consider joining a guided tour led by knowledgeable local guides or audio guides available for rent on-site. Guided tours often provide insights and anecdotes that enhance the visitor experience.

Palermo Cathedral stands as a symbol of Sicily's rich cultural heritage and serves as a captivating testament to the city's centuries-old legacy. Whether you're drawn to its awe-inspiring architecture, religious significance, or historical intrigue, a visit to Palermo Cathedral promises to be a memorable and enriching experience for travelers of all ages.

Norman Palace and Palatine Chapel:
Witness Magnificent History

The Norman Palace, also known as the Palazzo dei Normanni, stands as an architectural gem and a living testament to the rich history of Palermo. This historic palace, perched on the highest point of the ancient city, has been witness to centuries of political intrigue, cultural exchange, and architectural splendor.

History and Architecture:

Originally built in the 9th century during Arab rule, the Norman Palace underwent significant transformations under the Norman kings, particularly Roger II. The structure reflects a fascinating blend of Arab, Norman, and later Gothic influences, creating a unique architectural ensemble that captures the essence of Sicily's diverse cultural heritage.

The highlight of the Norman Palace is undoubtedly the Palatine Chapel, a jewel of medieval art and a UNESCO World Heritage Site. Commissioned by Roger II in the 12th century, the chapel is a masterpiece of Arab-Norman architecture, featuring a breathtaking fusion of Byzantine mosaics, Islamic geometric patterns, and Latin Christian iconography. The intricate mosaics depict biblical scenes, saints, and rulers, creating a visual narrative that transcends religious and cultural boundaries.

Visitors to the Palatine Chapel are often awe-struck by the shimmering golden mosaics that adorn the walls, ceilings, and dome. The mosaic of Christ Pantocrator, surrounded by angels, apostles, and saints, is particularly striking and exemplifies the skillful craftsmanship and artistic collaboration that characterized Sicily's Norman era.

Must-See Attractions:

The Royal Apartments: Within the Norman Palace complex, visitors can explore the Royal Apartments, which showcase a blend of medieval and Renaissance styles. The apartments feature elaborately decorated rooms, including the King's Chamber, the Hall of Roger II, and the Sala di

Ruggero, each offering insights into the courtly life of Sicily's rulers.

The Cappella Palatina: Adjacent to the Palatine Chapel, the Cappella Palatina is another religious sanctuary within the Norman Palace. This chapel, with its elegant arches, intricate stonework, and subdued color palette, provides a serene and contemplative space for visitors.

The Royal Palace Grounds: Beyond the architectural wonders, the Norman Palace is surrounded by lush gardens and courtyards that offer a tranquil escape from the bustling city. Visitors can stroll through well-manicured gardens, admire ornate fountains, and enjoy panoramic views of Palermo.

Visiting Tips:

Combined Tickets: Consider purchasing a combined ticket that allows access to both the Norman Palace and the nearby Palermo Cathedral. This can be a cost-effective way to explore multiple historic sites in a single visit.

Guided Tours: To gain a deeper understanding of the history, art, and architecture of the Norman Palace and Palatine Chapel, consider joining a guided tour. Knowledgeable guides can provide context to the intricate details and historical significance of these landmarks.

Opening Hours: The Norman Palace and Palatine Chapel have specific opening hours, and it's advisable to check in advance, especially during holidays or special events, to ensure that you can explore these treasures at your own pace.

Teatro Massimo: Experience Grandeur in Europe's Third Largest Opera House

Teatro Massimo, the grand opera house of Palermo, stands as a symbol of cultural sophistication and architectural splendor. As the third-largest opera house in Europe, this majestic venue not only hosts world-class performances but also invites visitors to immerse themselves in the opulence and grandeur of Sicily's artistic heritage.

History and Architecture:

Constructed in the late 19th century during a period of economic prosperity in Palermo, Teatro Massimo was designed by the renowned Italian architect Giovan Battista Filippo Basile. The opera house reflects the eclectic style of the time, blending Neoclassical and eclectic elements, with a monumental neoclassical façade adorned with statues and Corinthian columns.

The interiors of Teatro Massimo are equally impressive, featuring a vast auditorium with seating for over 3,000 spectators. The richly decorated ceilings, gilded ornaments, and intricate frescoes create an ambiance of luxury and refinement. The opera house has played a crucial role in shaping

Palermo's cultural identity, hosting performances ranging from opera and ballet to symphony concerts and theatrical productions.

Must-See Attractions:

The Main Auditorium: The heart of Teatro Massimo is its main auditorium, a space designed for both acoustic excellence and visual splendor. The horseshoe-shaped seating arrangement provides an intimate setting for audience members, ensuring an immersive experience during performances.

The Royal Box: Positioned prominently within the auditorium, the Royal Box is a regal space adorned with opulent decorations and luxurious furnishings. This exclusive area was historically reserved for royalty and distinguished guests attending performances at Teatro Massimo.

The Roof Terrace: For a unique perspective of Palermo and its surrounding landscapes, visitors can ascend to the roof terrace of Teatro Massimo. The terrace offers panoramic views of the city, the historic district, and the picturesque mountains in the distance.

Opera Performances and Events:

Teatro Massimo's reputation as a world-class venue is further enhanced by its diverse program of opera performances, ballets, and concerts. The opera house has hosted renowned artists and orchestras, contributing to Palermo's standing in the international cultural scene.

Visitors have the opportunity to attend scheduled performances, ranging from classic operas by composers such as Verdi and Puccini to contemporary works and ballet productions. The calendar of events is curated to appeal to a broad audience, ensuring that both seasoned opera enthusiasts and newcomers can enjoy a memorable cultural experience.

Visiting Tips:

Guided Tours: Teatro Massimo offers guided tours that provide in-depth insights into the history, architecture, and behind-the-scenes workings of the opera house. Guided tours often include access to areas not open to the general public, offering a comprehensive understanding of this cultural landmark.

Performance Tickets: If your visit coincides with a scheduled performance, consider purchasing tickets in advance to secure your seat. Attending a live performance at Teatro Massimo is a unique and unforgettable experience that allows you to appreciate the grandeur of the venue while enjoying world-class artistic presentations.

Photography: While exploring Teatro Massimo, photography is typically allowed in designated areas, such as the foyer and the roof terrace. However, it's advisable to check the specific photography policies during guided tours or performances to ensure compliance with the venue's regulations.

The Norman Palace and Palatine Chapel offer a captivating journey through the layers of Sicily's history, showcasing the artistic and cultural influences that have shaped the region. On the other hand, Teatro Massimo stands as a testament to Palermo's commitment to the arts, inviting visitors to experience the grandeur of opera within the splendid confines of one of Europe's largest and most renowned opera houses. Together, these attractions paint a vivid picture of Palermo's rich tapestry of heritage, seamlessly blending the ancient and the modern in a city that continues to captivate visitors from around the world.

Ballarò Market: Immerse Yourself in Palermo's Bustling Street Life

Ballarò Market stands as a vibrant symbol of Palermo's lively street culture and culinary traditions. Located in the heart of the historic district, this bustling market offers visitors a sensory overload of sights, sounds, and aromas, as well as a fascinating glimpse into the daily lives of Palermo's residents.

History and Atmosphere:

Dating back to the Arab period of Palermo's history, Ballarò Market has been a hub of commerce and community for centuries. The market's name is believed to be derived from the Arabic word "balhar," meaning "open-air market," reflecting its origins as a bustling trading center.

Today, Ballarò Market continues to thrive as a lively and chaotic marketplace, where vendors hawk a dizzying array of fresh produce, seafood, meats, cheeses, spices, and other local specialties. The narrow streets are lined with colorful stalls and awnings, creating a kaleidoscope of sights and sounds that can be overwhelming yet exhilarating for visitors.

Must-See Highlights:

Fresh Produce Stalls: One of the highlights of Ballarò Market is its vibrant selection of fresh fruits and vegetables, sourced from local farms and producers. Visitors can sample seasonal delights such as ripe tomatoes, fragrant citrus fruits, plump olives, and aromatic herbs, while soaking in the bustling atmosphere of the market.

Seafood Stands: Palermo's proximity to the Mediterranean Sea ensures a bounty of fresh seafood at Ballarò Market. From succulent fish and shellfish to octopus, squid, and swordfish, seafood enthusiasts will delight in the variety and quality of offerings available at the market's seafood stalls.

Street Food Vendors: For a taste of authentic Sicilian street food, visitors can indulge in a culinary adventure at Ballarò Market. From savory arancini (rice balls) and panelle (chickpea fritters) to sweet cannoli and granita, the market offers a tempting array of treats to satisfy every palate.

Tips for Visiting:

Timing: Ballarò Market is typically busiest in the mornings, especially on weekends, when locals and tourists flock to the market to shop for fresh ingredients and socialize. For a more relaxed experience, consider visiting during the early afternoon or weekday mornings.

Exploring: To fully immerse yourself in the vibrant atmosphere of Ballarò Market, take your time wandering through the labyrinthine streets and alleys, exploring the diverse array of stalls and interacting with vendors. Don't be afraid to haggle and negotiate prices, as it's all part of the market experience.

Safety: While Ballarò Market is generally safe for visitors, it's advisable to exercise caution and keep an eye on your belongings, especially in crowded areas. Be mindful of pickpockets and stay alert in crowded or congested areas of the market.

Ballarò Market offers a captivating blend of history, culture, and culinary delights, providing visitors with an authentic taste of Palermo's vibrant street life. Whether you're shopping for fresh ingredients, sampling Sicilian street food, or simply soaking in the bustling atmosphere, a visit to Ballarò Market promises to be a memorable and enriching experience.

Quattro Canti: Admire Baroque Splendor in Palermo's Historic Intersection

Quattro Canti, also known as Piazza Vigliena, is a magnificent Baroque square that serves as the focal point of Palermo's historic center. This stunning intersection, characterized by its elegant architecture, ornate facades, and grandiose statues, embodies the splendor and opulence of Sicily's Baroque era.

History and Architecture:

Constructed in the early 17th century under the patronage of the Spanish viceroys, Quattro Canti was designed as a grandiose urban planning project to celebrate the unity and prosperity of Palermo. The square takes its name from its distinctive shape, consisting of four identical segments that intersect at right angles, forming an octagonal space.

Each of the four segments of Quattro Canti is adorned with a monumental Baroque facade, featuring elaborate decorations, statues, and reliefs that depict allegorical figures, mythological scenes, and historical events. The facades are crowned by ornate pediments and surmounted by statues representing the four seasons, the four Spanish kings of Sicily, and various patron saints.

Symbolism and Significance:

Quattro Canti serves as a symbolic and cultural landmark in Palermo, representing the city's rich history, artistic heritage, and multicultural influences. The square's Baroque architecture reflects the prevailing aesthetic and artistic tastes of the period, characterized by exuberance, theatricality, and grandeur.

Beyond its architectural significance, Quattro Canti also holds historical and social significance as a gathering place and crossroads of commerce, culture, and civic life. Over the centuries, the square has witnessed triumphal processions, religious festivals, political demonstrations, and everyday activities, making it a vibrant and dynamic hub of activity.

Must-See Attractions:

Facade Details: Take the time to admire the intricate details and decorative elements of each facade at Quattro Canti, including the sculpted figures, ornamental motifs, and symbolic imagery. Each facade tells a story, reflecting the values, aspirations, and identity of Palermo's inhabitants.

Statues and Sculptures: Pay close attention to the statues and sculptures that adorn the upper levels of the facades, representing allegorical figures, mythological deities, and historical personalities. These sculptural elements add depth and dimension to the architectural ensemble, inviting contemplation and interpretation.

Surrounding Architecture: Beyond Quattro Canti itself, take the opportunity to explore the surrounding streets and alleys, which are lined with historic buildings, churches, and palaces. This area of Palermo's historic center is teeming with architectural treasures and hidden gems waiting to be discovered.

Visiting Tips:

Photography: Quattro Canti is a photographer's paradise, offering endless opportunities for capturing stunning architectural details and striking compositions. Whether you're using a professional camera or a smartphone, be sure to take plenty of photos to document your visit and preserve the memories.

Guided Tours: To gain a deeper understanding of the history, symbolism, and significance of Quattro Canti, consider joining a guided walking tour led by knowledgeable local guides. Guided tours provide insights and anecdotes that enhance the visitor experience, allowing you to appreciate the square's beauty and heritage from a new perspective.

Timing: Quattro Canti is particularly enchanting in the early morning or late afternoon, when the sunlight casts a warm glow on the facades and illuminates the intricate details of the sculptures and reliefs. Avoid visiting during midday when the square may be crowded and the sun is at its strongest.

Quattro Canti stands as a masterpiece of Baroque architecture and urban planning, offering visitors a glimpse into the grandeur and elegance of Palermo's historic past. Whether you're admiring the ornate facades, exploring the surrounding streets, or simply soaking in the atmosphere of this iconic square, a visit to Quattro Canti is sure to leave a lasting impression.

Mondello Beach: Relax and Unwind on Sicily's Stunning Coastline

Nestled along the azure waters of the Tyrrhenian Sea lies Mondello Beach, a picturesque seaside paradise that beckons travelers seeking sun, sand, and relaxation. Located just a short drive from Palermo's city center, this idyllic coastal retreat offers pristine beaches, crystalline waters, and a range of recreational activities for visitors of all ages.

Scenic Beauty and Natural Wonders:

Mondello Beach is renowned for its stunning natural beauty, characterized by its golden sands, turquoise waters, and dramatic backdrop of rugged cliffs and verdant hills. The crescent-shaped bay is sheltered from strong currents and winds, making it an ideal spot for swimming, sunbathing, and water sports.

One of the most iconic features of Mondello Beach is its Art Nouveau pier, which extends into the sea and offers panoramic views of the coastline. The pier is a popular gathering place for locals and tourists alike, providing a scenic vantage point for admiring the sunset or simply taking a leisurely stroll along the promenade.

Recreational Activities and Amenities:

Mondello Beach caters to outdoor enthusiasts with a wide range of recreational activities and amenities. Whether you're looking to soak up the sun on the sandy shores, cool off with a refreshing swim in the crystal-clear waters, or try your hand at water sports such as windsurfing, sailing, or paddleboarding, there's something for everyone to enjoy.

The beach is dotted with beach clubs, cafes, and restaurants offering umbrellas, sun loungers, and beachside service, allowing visitors to relax and unwind in comfort. Families with children will appreciate the shallow waters and gentle waves, which provide a safe and enjoyable environment for kids to splash and play.

Cultural and Culinary Delights:

In addition to its natural attractions, Mondello Beach offers opportunities to experience Sicilian culture and cuisine. Visitors can sample fresh seafood delicacies at beachside restaurants and trattorias, savoring the flavors of Sicilian cuisine while enjoying panoramic views of the sea.

Nearby attractions include the charming village of Mondello, with its colorful houses, quaint streets, and lively piazza. Visitors can explore the local shops, markets, and gelaterias, indulging in sweet treats such as granita and cannoli, traditional Sicilian desserts that are sure to satisfy any sweet tooth.

Visiting Tips:

Transportation: Mondello Beach is easily accessible from Palermo's city center by car, taxi, or public transportation. Parking can be limited during peak season, so it's advisable to arrive early or use alternative transportation options such as buses or bicycles.

Sun Protection: With its sunny climate and clear skies, Mondello Beach is the perfect place to soak up the sun. Be sure to pack sunscreen, hats, sunglasses, and plenty of water to stay hydrated and protected from the sun's rays, especially during the hottest hours of the day.

Beach Etiquette: Respect the natural environment and local customs by disposing of trash properly, respecting wildlife, and following any posted rules or regulations. Keep noise levels to a minimum and be mindful of other beachgoers, ensuring a pleasant and enjoyable experience for everyone.

Mondello Beach offers a blissful escape from the hustle and bustle of city life, providing visitors with a tranquil oasis of sun, sand, and sea. Whether you're seeking relaxation, adventure, or simply a taste of Sicilian coastal culture, a visit to Mondello Beach is sure to rejuvenate the body, mind, and spirit.

CHAPTER 3:
CULTURAL AND CULINARY DELIGHTS

Cultural and Culinary Delights invites you to embark on a sensory journey through the vibrant tapestry of Palermo's rich cultural heritage and mouth watering culinary scene. From savoring traditional Sicilian dishes at local trattorias to exploring the city's dynamic street art and partaking in colorful festivals, this chapter offers a tantalizing glimpse into the heart and soul of Palermo's cultural and gastronomic treasures. Discover the flavors, sights, and sounds that make Palermo a feast for the senses, and immerse yourself in the vibrant spirit of Sicilian culture and cuisine.

Best Restaurants in Palermo

Palermo's culinary scene is a vibrant tapestry of flavors, influenced by centuries of cultural exchange and culinary tradition. From traditional trattorias serving Sicilian specialties to innovative eateries reinterpreting classic dishes, the city offers a wealth of dining options to suit every palate and budget.

Fine Dining Establishments:

Ristorante Gagini: Tucked away in the heart of Palermo's historic center, Ristorante Gagini is renowned for its elegant ambiance and exquisite Sicilian cuisine. Helmed by acclaimed chef Pietro D'Agostino, the restaurant offers a seasonal menu that showcases the freshest local ingredients, prepared with precision and creativity. Signature dishes include arancini stuffed with creamy burrata, pasta with fresh seafood, and tender veal medallions with Marsala wine sauce.

Osteria dei Vespri: Situated near the iconic Quattro Canti, Osteria dei Vespri is a charming trattoria known for its rustic charm and hearty Sicilian fare. The menu features traditional dishes inspired by regional culinary traditions, such as pasta alla norma, caponata, and grilled swordfish with citrus salsa. It's popular among both residents and tourists because of the welcoming atmosphere and excellent service.

Street Food Gems:

Pane e Panelle: For a taste of authentic Sicilian street food, head to Pane e Panelle, a humble eatery specializing in panelle, chickpea fritters, and pani ca' meusa, spleen sandwiches. Served on freshly baked bread and seasoned with lemon juice and salt, these savory snacks are a beloved staple of Palermo's culinary heritage.

Focacceria San Francesco: A Palermo institution since 1834, Focacceria San Francesco is famous for its mouthwatering selection of Sicilian street food classics. From savory sfincione, a thick-crust pizza topped with onions, tomatoes, and anchovies, to crisp arancine stuffed with ragu or spinach and ricotta, every bite is a celebration of Sicilian flavors and traditions.

Hidden Gems:

Trattoria da Pino: Tucked away in the back streets of Palermo's Kalsa district, Trattoria da Pino is a hidden gem beloved by locals for its homestyle cooking and warm hospitality. The menu features an array of Sicilian specialties, including pasta con le sarde, a savory pasta dish with sardines, wild fennel, and pine nuts, and involtini di pesce spada, swordfish rolls stuffed with breadcrumbs, herbs, and cheese.

Antica Focacceria San Francesco: Founded in 1834, Antica Focacceria San Francesco is a historic eatery known for its traditional Sicilian fare and atmospheric dining rooms adorned with vintage photos and memorabilia. Specialties include pasta con le sarde, caponata, and the restaurant's namesake dish, focaccia topped with tomato, onion, and cheese.

Visiting Tips:

Reservations: For popular restaurants and fine dining establishments, it's advisable to make reservations in advance, especially during peak tourist seasons or on weekends.

Local Recommendations: Don't hesitate to ask locals or hotel staff for recommendations on where to dine in Palermo. They often have insider tips and hidden gems that may not be found in guidebooks or online reviews.

Exploration: Take the opportunity to explore different neighborhoods and districts of Palermo, as each area offers its own unique culinary delights and dining experiences. From bustling markets to quaint trattorias, the city is a treasure trove of gastronomic delights waiting to be discovered.

Palermo's dining scene is a testament to the city's rich culinary heritage and diverse cultural influences. Whether you're savoring traditional Sicilian dishes at a family-run trattoria or indulging in innovative cuisine at a fine dining restaurant, every meal is an opportunity to experience the flavors and traditions of this captivating city.

Street Food Safari: Indulge in Palermo's Gastronomic Treasures

Palermo's street food scene is a gastronomic adventure waiting to be explored, offering a tantalizing array of savory snacks, sweet treats, and culinary delights served up fresh and flavorful by street vendors and hole-in-the-wall eateries. From iconic classics like arancini and sfincione to lesser-known gems like panelle and crocchè, a street food safari through Palermo promises to be a feast for the senses.

Arancini:

One of Palermo's most iconic street foods, arancini are golden-fried rice balls filled with a variety of savory fillings, such as ragu, cheese, peas, and saffron. The name "arancini" is derived from the Italian word for "little oranges," owing to their round shape and golden hue. These delicious snacks are perfect for on-the-go eating and can be found at street food stalls, bakeries, and cafes throughout the city.

Sfincione:

Sfincione is a traditional Sicilian street food that bears resemblance to pizza but with a thicker crust and a unique topping of tomatoes, onions, anchovies, and breadcrumbs. The dough is allowed to rise slowly, resulting in a light and airy texture, while the savory toppings impart a burst of flavor with every bite. Sfincione is typically sold by the slice and is a popular choice for a quick and satisfying snack.

Panelle:

Panelle are deep-fried chickpea fritters that are a beloved staple of Palermo's street food scene. Made from a simple batter of chickpea flour, water, and salt, panelle is fried until golden and crispy, then served hot with a sprinkle of salt and a squeeze of lemon juice. These savory snacks are popular with locals and visitors alike and can be enjoyed on their own or sandwiched between slices of freshly baked bread.

Crocchè:

Crocchè, or potato croquettes, are another popular street food in Palermo, featuring creamy mashed potatoes seasoned with herbs and spices, then breaded and fried until crispy. The result is a crunchy exterior that gives way to a soft and fluffy interior, bursting with flavor. Crocchè are often served as a snack or appetizer, either on their own or accompanied by a dollop of aioli or marinara sauce for dipping.

Palermo's street food safari offers a tantalizing glimpse into the city's culinary heritage and cultural identity, inviting visitors to embark on a flavorful journey through its bustling streets and vibrant markets. Whether you're savoring a crispy arancino, biting into a slice of sfincione, or munching on a hot panelle, every taste is a celebration of Palermo's rich gastronomic tradition.

Palermo Street Art: Explore Vibrant Murals and Graffiti

Palermo's streets are a canvas for artistic expression, adorned with vibrant murals, colorful graffiti, and thought-provoking street art that reflects the city's cultural diversity, social issues, and creative spirit. From large-scale murals that dominate building facades to hidden gems tucked away in narrow alleyways, Palermo's street art scene offers a visual feast for art lovers and urban explorers alike.

History and Evolution:

The tradition of street art in Palermo dates back decades, with graffiti emerging as a form of protest and political expression during periods of social unrest and economic hardship. Over time, street art has evolved into a recognized and respected art form, attracting local and international artists who contribute to the city's ever-changing urban landscape.

Today, Palermo's street art scene encompasses a diverse range of styles, techniques, and themes, from abstract murals and geometric patterns to figurative portraits and surreal landscapes. Artists draw inspiration from a variety of sources, including Sicilian folklore, historical events, contemporary issues, and personal experiences, resulting in a dynamic and eclectic collection of artworks that reflect the city's cultural richness and complexity.

Exploring Street Art Hotspots:

Vucciria Market: Located in the heart of Palermo's historic center, Vucciria Market is a bustling hub of activity and a hotspot for street art enthusiasts. Wander through the narrow streets and alleys surrounding the market, where colorful murals and graffiti adorn building facades, doorways, and shop shutters, creating a vibrant backdrop for the bustling marketplace.

Kalsa District: The Kalsa district is a treasure trove of street art, with its labyrinthine streets and historic buildings providing the perfect canvas for artistic expression. Explore the neighborhood's hidden corners and quiet alleyways, where you'll discover an array of murals, stencils, and paste-ups that reflect the area's rich cultural heritage and bohemian atmosphere.

Notable Artworks and Artists:

Blu: Renowned Italian street artist Blu has left his mark on Palermo's urban landscape with a series of striking murals that explore themes of social justice, environmental activism, and human rights. His larger-than-life creations can be found on buildings and walls throughout the city, offering poignant commentary on contemporary issues and global challenges.

Alice Pasquini: Rome-based artist Alice Pasquini is known for her whimsical and colorful murals that depict scenes of everyday life and human interaction. Her works can be found in neighborhoods across Palermo, brightening up neglected spaces and sparking conversations about community, belonging, and the human experience.

Palermo's street art scene is a dynamic and ever-evolving reflection of the city's cultural diversity, social dynamics, and creative energy. Whether you're admiring a monumental mural, deciphering a cryptic stencil, or simply soaking in the vibrant atmosphere of the urban landscape, exploring Palermo's street art is a journey of discovery and inspiration.

Traditional Festivals: Participate in Colorful Celebrations and Religious Events

Palermo's calendar is dotted with a colorful array of traditional festivals, religious processions, and cultural celebrations that showcase the city's rich heritage, vibrant traditions, and strong sense of community. From religious feasts and folklore festivals to music concerts and street parades, there's always something happening in Palermo to delight and entertain visitors of all ages.

Religious Festivals:

Santa Rosalia Festival: The Feast of Santa Rosalia, the patron saint of Palermo, is one of the city's most beloved and anticipated events, celebrated annually in July. The festival honors the miraculous intercession of Santa Rosalia, who is credited with saving Palermo from the plague in the 17th century. Highlights of the festival include religious processions, street fairs, fireworks displays, and the iconic "Acchianata" procession, in which the statue of Santa Rosalia is carried through the streets of Palermo in a grand procession.

Holy Week Processions: During Holy Week, Palermo comes alive with a series of solemn processions and religious rituals commemorating the Passion, Death, and Resurrection of Jesus Christ. Elaborate floats adorned with statues depicting scenes from the Bible are carried through the streets by members of religious brotherhoods, accompanied by marching bands, penitents, and worshippers dressed in traditional attire. The processions culminate in the Good Friday procession, known as the "Processione dei Misteri," which retraces the Stations of the Cross and attracts thousands of spectators.

Folklore Festivals:

Festival of Saint Agatha: The Festival of Saint Agatha, held annually in February, is one of the most important religious events in Palermo, commemorating the martyrdom of Saint Agatha, the city's co-patron saint. The festival features religious processions, street decorations, and culinary traditions, including the iconic "cassatelle," sweet pastries filled with ricotta cheese and chocolate chips, which are traditionally eaten during the festivities.

Festival of Saint Rosalia in Monte Pellegrino: The Festival of Saint Rosalia in Monte Pellegrino is a centuries-old tradition that takes place in September, celebrating the life and miracles of the patron saint of Palermo. The festival includes religious ceremonies, musical performances, and cultural events, culminating in a pilgrimage to the sanctuary of Santa Rosalia atop Monte Pellegrino, where worshippers pay homage to the saint and seek her intercession.

Music and Cultural Events:

Festival delle Sagre: The Festival delle Sagre, held annually in September, is a celebration of Sicilian cuisine, music, and culture, showcasing the culinary traditions of Palermo and the surrounding regions. The festival features food stalls offering a variety of local specialties, live music performances, dance demonstrations, and artisanal crafts, providing visitors with a taste of Sicily's rich cultural heritage.

Teatro Massimo Summer Opera Season: The Teatro Massimo, Europe's third-largest opera house, hosts a prestigious summer opera season from June to August, featuring world-class performances of operas, ballets, and classical concerts. The season attracts opera aficionados from around the world who come to experience the grandeur and splendor of Palermo's cultural scene in one of its most iconic venues.

Visiting Tips:

Planning Ahead: Check the local events calendar and plan your visit to coincide with one of Palermo's traditional festivals or cultural events to experience the city's vibrant atmosphere and rich heritage firsthand.

Respect for Traditions: Show respect for local customs and traditions by observing the rituals and ceremonies associated with religious festivals, such as processions and church services. Dress modestly and refrain from disruptive behavior during religious events out of respect for worshippers and participants.

Participation: Don't be afraid to immerse yourself in the festivities and participate in the cultural activities and rituals that characterize Palermo's traditional festivals. Whether it's sampling traditional foods, joining a procession, or watching a folk dance performance, engaging with the local community is a rewarding way to experience the city's cultural heritage.

Safety and Security: Be mindful of your personal safety and security, especially in crowded areas during large-scale events and celebrations. Keep your belongings secure and stay alert to your surroundings to avoid potential risks or incidents.

Palermo's traditional festivals offer a glimpse into the city's rich cultural heritage, religious traditions, and community spirit, providing visitors with an unforgettable opportunity to experience the sights, sounds, and flavors of Sicily's vibrant capital. Whether you're marveling at the elaborate processions of Holy Week, savoring the flavors of the Santa Rosalia Festival, or dancing the night away at the Festival delle Sagre, each festival is a celebration of Palermo's unique identity and timeless charm.

CHAPTER 4:
DAY TRIPS AND EXCURSIONS

Palermo's strategic location in the heart of Sicily makes it an ideal base for exploring the island's diverse landscapes, historic sites, and cultural attractions. From majestic cathedrals and charming seaside towns to rugged mountains and active volcanoes, there are countless day trip options waiting to be discovered just a short distance from the city center. Whether you're seeking cultural enrichment, outdoor adventure, or simply a change of scenery, these day trips offer a memorable escape from the hustle and bustle of urban life.

Monreale: Visit the Majestic Cathedral and Benedictine Cloister

Just a short drive from Palermo lies the picturesque town of Monreale, home to one of Sicily's most magnificent treasures: the Duomo di Monreale, or Monreale Cathedral. Built in the 12th century by Norman kings, this UNESCO World Heritage Site is renowned for its stunning Byzantine mosaics, intricate architecture, and rich history.

Monreale Cathedral:

The centerpiece of Monreale's architectural ensemble, the cathedral boasts a grand facade adorned with intricate carvings, marble columns, and bronze doors depicting scenes from the Old and New Testaments. Step inside to marvel at the cathedral's awe-inspiring interior, where thousands of square meters of shimmering mosaics cover the walls, depicting biblical stories, saints, and celestial beings in vivid detail.

Benedictine Cloister:

Adjacent to the cathedral is the Benedictine Cloister, a tranquil oasis of greenery and serenity that offers respite from the bustling streets of Monreale. Built in the 12th century, the cloister is renowned for its graceful arcades, slender columns, and intricately carved capitals, which feature a rich variety of decorative motifs and symbols. Take a leisurely stroll through the cloister's shaded garden, admiring the delicate interplay of light and shadow cast by the slender columns and lush foliage.

Visiting Tips:

Transportation: Monreale is easily accessible from Palermo by car, taxi, or public transportation. The journey takes approximately 20-30 minutes by road, depending on traffic conditions. Alternatively, guided tours and organized excursions are available for visitors who prefer a hassle-free travel experience.

Opening Hours: Monreale Cathedral and the Benedictine Cloister are typically open to visitors daily, with varying opening hours throughout the year. It's advisable to check the official website or inquire locally for the most up-to-date information on opening hours, admission fees, and any special events or exhibitions.

Attire: As Monreale Cathedral is a sacred place of worship, visitors are requested to dress modestly and respectfully. Avoid wearing revealing clothing or beach attire, and consider covering your shoulders and knees as a sign of respect for religious customs and traditions.

Guided Tours: For a more immersive experience, consider joining a guided tour of Monreale Cathedral and the Benedictine Cloister, led by knowledgeable local guides who can provide insights into the history, architecture, and significance of these historic landmarks. Guided tours may include skip-the-line access, allowing you to bypass queues and maximize your time exploring the sites.

A visit to Monreale offers a captivating journey through Sicily's rich cultural heritage and architectural splendor, where centuries of history and craftsmanship come to life in a dazzling display of artistry and devotion. Whether you're admiring the shimmering mosaics of the cathedral or finding solace in the tranquil beauty of the cloister, Monreale promises an unforgettable day trip filled with wonder and discovery.

Cefalù: Explore Charming Seaside Town with a Picturesque Historic Center

Nestled along the northern coast of Sicily, just a scenic drive from Palermo, lies the charming seaside town of Cefalù. Blessed with a picturesque setting, a rich history, and a vibrant cultural scene, Cefalù beckons travelers with its enchanting blend of natural beauty and architectural splendor.

Historic Center:

The heart of Cefalù is its historic center, a maze of narrow streets, cobblestone alleys, and medieval buildings that exude old-world charm and timeless elegance. Wander through the labyrinthine streets of the centro storico, where colorful facades, wrought-iron balconies, and ancient churches create a captivating tableau of Sicilian life and culture.

Cefalù Cathedral:

Dominating the skyline of Cefalù is its crowning jewel, the majestic Cefalù Cathedral, a UNESCO World Heritage Site renowned for its stunning architecture and exquisite mosaics. Built in the 12th century by Norman kings, the cathedral boasts a monumental facade adorned with twin towers, intricate carvings, and a magnificent rose window that bathes the interior in a kaleidoscope of colored light.

La Rocca:

For panoramic views of Cefalù and the surrounding coastline, hike to the top of La Rocca, a towering limestone promontory that overlooks the town. The climb to the summit is rewarded with breathtaking vistas of the Tyrrhenian Sea, the rugged coastline, and the red-tiled rooftops of Cefalù below. Along the way, pass by ancient ruins, lush vegetation, and hidden caves that speak to the island's ancient past.

Visiting Tips:

Transportation: Cefalù is easily accessible from Palermo by car, bus, or train, with the journey taking approximately one hour by road or rail. Parking can be limited in the town center, especially during peak tourist seasons, so it's advisable to arrive early or use public transportation to avoid parking hassles.

Sightseeing: Take the time to explore Cefalù at your own pace, allowing yourself to wander through its winding streets and discover hidden gems around every corner. Don't miss the opportunity to explore the town's charming shops, quaint cafes, and artisan workshops, where you can sample local delicacies and purchase handmade souvenirs to commemorate your visit.

Beach Time: After exploring the town center, head to Cefalù's sandy beaches to relax and unwind by the sparkling waters of the Tyrrhenian Sea. Whether you prefer lounging on the shore, swimming in the sea, or trying your hand at water sports such as windsurfing or paddleboarding, Cefalù's beaches offer something for everyone to enjoy.

Cultural Experiences: Immerse yourself in Cefalù's vibrant cultural scene by attending a concert, art exhibition, or theatrical performance at one of the town's cultural venues. From outdoor concerts in the piazza to gallery openings in historic palazzi, there's always something happening in Cefalù to delight and inspire visitors of all ages.

Cefalù's timeless beauty and relaxed atmosphere make it the perfect destination for a day trip from Palermo, offering a harmonious blend of history, culture, and natural splendor that captivates the senses and nourishes the soul. Whether you're marveling at the mosaics of the cathedral, strolling along the seafront promenade, or soaking up the sun on the beach, a day in Cefalù promises an unforgettable experience filled with joy and wonder.

Mount Etna: Embark on an Adventure to Europe's Most Active Volcano

Rising majestically above the eastern coast of Sicily, Mount Etna is one of the most iconic landmarks of the Mediterranean, a towering symbol of natural beauty and geological wonder. As Europe's highest and most active volcano, Mount Etna offers a thrilling day trip opportunity for adventurous travelers seeking to explore its otherworldly landscapes, volcanic craters, and lunar-like terrain.

Volcanic Landscapes:

Embark on a scenic drive from Palermo to Mount Etna, passing through picturesque villages, verdant vineyards, and rugged countryside along the way. As you approach the volcano, the landscape gradually transforms into a surreal panorama of lava fields, volcanic cones, and barren slopes, revealing the awesome power and beauty of nature in its rawest form.

Crater Exploration:

Once at Mount Etna, take the opportunity to explore its volcanic craters and lava flows up close, either on foot or by cable car and off-road vehicle. Guided tours and excursions are available for visitors of all fitness levels, allowing you to hike to the summit, descend into crater valleys, and witness the geothermal activity and steaming vents that characterize the volcano's ever-changing landscape.

Silvestri Craters:

For a less strenuous excursion, visit the Silvestri Craters, a series of dormant volcanic cones located on the southern slopes of Mount Etna. Accessible by road, the Silvestri Craters offer panoramic views of the surrounding countryside and the smoking peak of the volcano, providing a fascinating glimpse into the geological forces that have shaped the island's landscape over millennia.

Visiting Tips:

Safety Precautions: Mount Etna is an active volcano, and conditions can change rapidly, so it's important to exercise caution and follow the guidance of trained guides and park rangers at all times. Wear sturdy footwear, dress in layers, and carry plenty of water and sunscreen to stay hydrated and protected from the elements.

Weather Conditions: The weather on Mount Etna can be unpredictable, with temperatures fluctuating dramatically and sudden changes in visibility due to fog, clouds, or volcanic emissions. Check the weather forecast and volcanic activity reports before setting out on your excursion, and be prepared to adjust your plans accordingly based on current conditions.

Altitude Considerations: Mount Etna's summit reaches an elevation of over 3,300 meters (10,800 feet), so visitors should be mindful of the effects of altitude and take precautions to prevent altitude sickness, such as taking breaks, staying hydrated, and avoiding strenuous activity if experiencing symptoms of altitude illness.

Guided Tours: Consider joining a guided tour or excursion led by experienced guides who can provide insights into the geology, history, and ecology of Mount Etna, as well as ensure your safety and well-being throughout the journey. Guided tours may include transportation, equipment rental, and expert commentary, allowing you to focus on enjoying the experience without worrying about logistics.

A visit to Mount Etna offers a once-in-a-lifetime opportunity to witness the awesome power of nature in action, as you explore its volcanic landscapes, geological wonders, and mystical allure. Whether you're hiking to the summit, marveling at the lava flows, or gazing out over the sweeping vistas of the Sicilian countryside, a day on Mount Etna promises an unforgettable adventure filled with excitement, wonder, and discovery.

CHAPTER 5:
SAMPLE ITINERARIES FOR DIFFERENT TRAVEL STYLES

Palermo, with its rich history, vibrant culture, and eclectic charm, offers something for every type of traveler, whether you're seeking a quick overview of the city's highlights, planning a comprehensive exploration over a weekend getaway, or embarking on a leisurely journey to discover its hidden gems. These sample itineraries are tailored to different travel styles, ensuring a memorable and fulfilling experience for visitors of all interests and preferences.

One Day in Palermo: Highlights for Short Stays

For travelers with limited time to spare, a day in Palermo offers a whirlwind tour of the city's most iconic landmarks, historic sites, and cultural attractions. From majestic cathedrals and bustling markets to tranquil gardens and panoramic viewpoints, this itinerary is designed to showcase the essence of Palermo in a single day, allowing you to make the most of your short stay in the Sicilian capital.

Morning:

Start at the Palermo Cathedral: Begin your day with a visit to the Palermo Cathedral, a masterpiece of Norman architecture and a symbol of the city's religious heritage. Marvel at its impressive facade, intricate mosaics, and ornate tombs, before ascending to the rooftop for panoramic views of the city and the surrounding mountains.

Explore the Ballarò Market: Immerse yourself in the sights, sounds, and smells of Palermo's vibrant street life at the Ballarò Market, one of the city's oldest and most bustling markets. Wander through its labyrinthine alleys, browsing stalls piled high with fresh produce, local delicacies, and artisanal crafts, and savoring the flavors of Sicilian street food.

Afternoon:

Visit the Norman Palace: Step back in time at the Norman Palace, the former royal residence of Sicily's Norman kings, and explore its opulent halls, lavish apartments, and exquisite mosaics. Don't miss the chance to admire the Palatine Chapel, a UNESCO World Heritage Site renowned for its dazzling Byzantine mosaics and golden ceiling.

Stroll through the Botanical Gardens: Escape the hustle and bustle of the city with a leisurely stroll through the Orto Botanico di Palermo, a tranquil oasis of greenery and serenity in the heart of Palermo. Explore its lush gardens, shaded pathways, and exotic plant collections, pausing to admire the colorful flowers, fragrant herbs, and towering trees.

Evening:

Dine at a Traditional Trattoria: Conclude your day with a delicious dinner at a traditional trattoria, where you can savor authentic Sicilian cuisine in a cozy and welcoming atmosphere. Indulge in local specialties such as pasta alla norma, arancini di riso, and cannoli siciliani, accompanied by a glass of Sicilian wine or a refreshing limoncello.

Enjoy an Evening Stroll: Take a leisurely evening stroll through the historic streets of Palermo, soaking up the ambiance of its illuminated squares, bustling piazzas, and lively nightlife. Admire the illuminated facades of landmarks such as the Teatro Massimo and the Quattro Canti, and mingle with locals and fellow travelers in the city's vibrant street cafes and bars.

Weekend Getaway: Comprehensive Exploration for Weekend Travelers

For travelers with a bit more time to spare, a weekend getaway in Palermo offers the perfect opportunity to delve deeper into the city's rich history, cultural heritage, and culinary delights. From guided tours and museum visits to leisurely strolls and scenic excursions, this itinerary is packed with experiences that showcase the best of what Palermo has to offer over a two-day period.

Day 1:

Morning:

Guided Walking Tour: Start your weekend getaway with a guided walking tour of Palermo's historic center, led by a knowledgeable local guide who can provide insights into the city's history, architecture, and culture. Explore landmarks such as the Palermo Cathedral, the Norman Palace, and the Church of San Giovanni degli Eremiti, learning about their significance and historical context.

Visit the Palermo Archaeological Museum: Dive into Sicily's ancient past with a visit to the Palermo Archaeological Museum, home to a vast collection of artifacts, sculptures, and archaeological finds dating back to ancient times. Marvel at the intricate details of Greek and Roman artifacts, Phoenician artifacts, and Egyptian artifacts, gaining a deeper understanding of Sicily's multicultural heritage.

Lunch at a Local Trattoria: Take a break from sightseeing with a leisurely lunch at a local trattoria, where you can sample traditional Sicilian dishes made with fresh, locally sourced ingredients. Indulge in specialties such as pasta con le sarde, caponata, and cassata siciliana, paired with a glass of Sicilian wine or a refreshing citrus granita.

Afternoon:

Explore the Capuchin Catacombs: Delve into the macabre side of Palermo's history with a visit to the Capuchin Catacombs, a fascinating underground labyrinth containing thousands of mummified remains dating back to the 16th century. Wander through its eerie corridors, crypts, and chapels, marveling at the preserved bodies and elaborate funerary decorations.

Discover the Teatro Massimo: Experience the grandeur and elegance of Europe's third-largest opera house with a guided tour of the Teatro Massimo, a magnificent neoclassical landmark that has been a cultural icon of Palermo since its inauguration in 1897. Admire its opulent interiors, majestic halls, and exquisite architectural details, and learn about its storied history and prestigious artistic legacy.

Day 2:

Morning:

Excursion to Monreale: Embark on a half-day excursion to the nearby town of Monreale, home to one of Sicily's most magnificent treasures: the Duomo di Monreale, or Monreale Cathedral. Marvel at its breathtaking mosaics, intricate architecture, and panoramic views of the Conca d'Oro valley, before exploring the town's charming streets, shops, and cafes at your leisure.

Visit the Benedictine Cloister: Adjacent to the cathedral is the Benedictine Cloister, a serene oasis of greenery and tranquility that offers respite from the hustle and bustle of urban life. Take a leisurely stroll through its shaded garden, admiring the graceful arcades, slender columns, and intricately carved capitals that adorn its tranquil courtyards.

Lunch in Monreale: Enjoy a leisurely lunch in Monreale at a local trattoria or cafe, where you can savor traditional Sicilian cuisine in a relaxed and welcoming atmosphere. Sample regional specialties such as panelle, arancini, and cannoli, accompanied by a glass of local wine or a refreshing Sicilian lemonade.

Afternoon:

Relax at Mondello Beach: Spend the afternoon soaking up the sun and sea at Mondello Beach, a picturesque seaside resort located just a short drive from Palermo. Lounge on its golden sands, swim in its crystal-clear waters, or indulge in water sports such as paddleboarding, windsurfing, or kayaking, enjoying the laid-back ambiance and stunning coastal scenery.

Dinner in Mondello: Conclude your weekend getaway with a romantic dinner at one of Mondello's waterfront restaurants, where you can dine al fresco overlooking the shimmering waters of the Mediterranean. Feast on fresh seafood, grilled fish, and Sicilian specialties, accompanied by a bottle of local wine and the gentle sea breeze.

Slow Travel Experience: Leisurely Discovering Palermo's Hidden Gems

For travelers who prefer to take their time and savor the journey, a slow travel experience in Palermo offers the opportunity to immerse yourself in the city's rich tapestry of culture, history, and everyday life. From leisurely walks and cultural experiences to culinary adventures and off-the-beaten-path discoveries, this itinerary is designed to unfold at a relaxed pace, allowing you to uncover Palermo's hidden gems and secret treasures at your own leisure.

Day 1:

Morning:

Explore the Historic Markets: Begin your slow travel experience with a leisurely stroll through Palermo's historic markets, where you can soak up the sights, sounds, and smells of daily life in the city. Wander through the bustling stalls of the Vucciria, Ballarò, and Capo markets, browsing for fresh produce, local specialties, and artisanal crafts, and chatting with friendly vendors and fellow shoppers along the way.

Visit the Palermo Botanical Gardens: Escape the urban hustle and bustle with a visit to the Orto

Botanico di Palermo, a peaceful oasis of greenery and tranquility nestled within the city center. Explore its lush gardens, shaded pathways, and exotic plant collections, discovering a diverse array of flora from around the world and enjoying the serenity of nature in the heart of Palermo.

Lunch at a Garden Cafe: Take a break from sightseeing with a leisurely lunch at a garden cafe or trattoria, where you can dine al fresco amidst the beauty of the botanical gardens. Enjoy seasonal dishes made with fresh, locally sourced ingredients, paired with a glass of Sicilian wine or a refreshing herbal infusion, and savor the flavors of Sicilian cuisine in a relaxed and peaceful setting.

Afternoon:

Discover Palermo's Street Art: Spend the afternoon exploring Palermo's vibrant street art scene, discovering colorful murals, graffiti, and urban installations hidden throughout the city's neighborhoods. Join a guided street art tour or simply wander at your own pace, admiring the creativity and talent of local artists as you uncover their works of art adorning walls, alleys, and public spaces.

Visit Contemporary Art Spaces: Dive deeper into Palermo's cultural landscape with a visit to its contemporary art spaces and galleries, where you can discover the latest trends and emerging talents in the city's vibrant art scene. Explore venues such as the Palazzo Riso, the Museo d'Arte Contemporanea della Sicilia, and the Fondazione Sant'Elia, discovering thought-provoking exhibitions, installations, and multimedia works by contemporary artists from Sicily and beyond.

Evening:

Dine at a Slow Food Restaurant: Conclude your day with a memorable dinner at a slow food restaurant, where you can savor the flavors of Sicilian cuisine in a relaxed and convivial atmosphere. Indulge in farm-to-table dishes made with organic, seasonal ingredients sourced from local farmers and producers, and enjoy the simple pleasures of good food, good company, and good conversation as you linger over a leisurely meal.

Enjoy an Evening Concert or Performance: Immerse yourself in Palermo's cultural scene with an evening concert or performance at one of the city's historic venues or contemporary spaces. From classical concerts and jazz performances to experimental theater and dance productions, there's always something happening in Palermo to delight and inspire cultural enthusiasts of all tastes and interests.

Day 2:

Morning:

Embark on a Historical Walking Tour: Start your second day with a leisurely historical walking tour of Palermo's lesser-known neighborhoods and hidden landmarks, guided by a local expert who can provide insights into the city's history, architecture, and cultural heritage. Explore off-the-beaten-path attractions such as the Kalsa district, the Zisa Castle, and the Church of Santa Maria dello Spasimo, discovering hidden gems and secret treasures that lie off the tourist trail.

Visit Artisan Workshops and Boutiques: Discover Palermo's vibrant artisanal traditions with a visit to its workshops and boutiques, where you can meet local artisans, craftsmen, and designers and learn about their traditional techniques and contemporary creations. Explore neighborhoods such as the Albergheria and the Vucciria, where you'll find a wealth of workshops specializing in ceramics, textiles, jewelry, and other handmade goods, and shop for unique souvenirs and gifts to take home as mementos of your slow travel experience in Palermo.

Lunch at a Family-Run Trattoria: Enjoy a leisurely lunch at a family-run trattoria or osteria, where you can dine like a local and experience the authentic flavors of Sicilian home cooking. Savor traditional dishes such as pasta al forno, panelle, and arancini, prepared with love and care by skilled chefs using time-honored recipes and fresh, locally sourced ingredients, and enjoy the warm hospitality and convivial atmosphere of a true Sicilian meal.

Afternoon:

Relax in a Historic Garden: Spend the afternoon unwinding in one of Palermo's historic gardens or green spaces, where you can escape the hustle and bustle of the city and enjoy moments of peace and tranquility amidst lush vegetation and scenic landscapes. Explore venues such as the Villa Giulia, the Villa Bonanno, and the Villa Trabia, discovering hidden oases of beauty and serenity that offer a welcome respite from the urban chaos.

Take a Leisurely Boat Tour: Embark on a leisurely boat tour of Palermo's coastline and harbor, exploring its picturesque bays, coves, and promenades from a unique perspective. Cruise past historic landmarks such as the Castello a Mare, the Foro Italico, and the Palazzo delle Aquile, and admire panoramic views of the city skyline and the sparkling waters of the Mediterranean as you relax and unwind on a scenic boat ride.

Evening:

Dine at a Seafront Ristorante: Conclude your slow travel experience with a romantic dinner at a seafront ristorante, where you can enjoy panoramic views of the sunset over the Mediterranean while savoring fresh seafood and regional specialties. Indulge in dishes such as grilled fish, seafood risotto, and spaghetti ai frutti di mare, accompanied by a bottle of local wine or prosecco, and toast to the memories of your leisurely exploration of Palermo's hidden gems and secret treasures.

A slow travel experience in Palermo invites you to embrace the art of leisure and discovery, as you immerse yourself in the rhythms of everyday life, savor the flavors of Sicilian cuisine, and uncover the city's hidden gems and secret treasures at your own pace. Whether you're exploring historic markets, discovering street art, or relaxing in a tranquil garden, each moment is an opportunity to connect with the soul of Palermo and create lasting memories of your journey through its vibrant streets and timeless landscapes.

CHAPTER 6:
ADDITIONAL RESOURCES AND
USEFUL CONTACTS

In your exploration of Palermo, it's essential to stay informed and prepared, ensuring a safe and enjoyable experience throughout your journey. This chapter provides valuable resources and contacts to help you navigate the city with confidence, from safety tips and local etiquette to tourist information centers and emergency contacts.

Safety Tips and Local Etiquette

Palermo is a vibrant and welcoming city, but like any urban area, it's important to stay vigilant and aware of your surroundings to ensure your safety and well-being. Here are some essential safety tips and local etiquette guidelines to keep in mind during your time in Palermo:

Stay Alert: Keep your belongings secure and be mindful of pickpockets, especially in crowded areas such as markets, public transportation, and tourist attractions. Carry only what you need and avoid displaying valuables openly.

Respect Local Customs: Palermo has a rich cultural heritage and strong sense of tradition, so it's important to respect local customs and etiquette. Dress modestly when visiting religious sites, cover your shoulders and knees, and remove your shoes before entering churches and mosques.

Use Caution at Night: While Palermo is generally safe for tourists, it's advisable to exercise caution when exploring the city after dark, especially in unfamiliar neighborhoods or isolated areas. Stick to well-lit streets and busy areas, and avoid walking alone late at night.

Be Aware of Traffic: Palermo's streets can be busy and chaotic, with heavy traffic and aggressive drivers, so exercise caution when crossing roads and navigating intersections. Use designated crosswalks, follow traffic signals, and be vigilant for speeding vehicles and erratic driving behavior.

Stay Hydrated: Sicily enjoys a warm Mediterranean climate, with hot summers and mild winters, so it's important to stay hydrated and protect yourself from the sun. Carry a reusable water bottle and drink plenty of fluids throughout the day, especially if you're out exploring in the heat.

Seek Local Advice: If you're unsure about safety or need assistance, don't hesitate to seek help from locals or authorities. Palermo's residents are known for their hospitality and willingness to assist visitors, so don't be afraid to ask for directions, recommendations, or assistance if needed.

By following these safety tips and respecting local customs, you can enjoy a safe and rewarding experience in Palermo, immersing yourself in the city's vibrant culture, history, and hospitality while minimizing any potential risks or challenges.

Tourist Information Centers

Tourist information centers are invaluable resources for travelers seeking assistance, guidance, and information about Palermo and its surrounding areas. These centers provide a wealth of resources, including maps, brochures, event schedules, and personalized recommendations to help you make the most of your visit. Here are some tourist information centers in Palermo:

APT Palermo - Tourist Information Office:
Address: Via Principe di Belmonte, 94, 90134 Palermo PA, Italy Phone: +39 091 6058351 Website: www.palermotourism.com

APT Palermo is the official tourist information office of Palermo, offering a range of services to assist visitors, including city maps, guided tours, hotel reservations, and event bookings. Knowledgeable staff are available to provide personalized recommendations and assistance in multiple languages.

Tourist Information Point - Piazza Verdi:
Address: Piazza Giuseppe Verdi, 90138 Palermo PA, Italy Phone: +39 091 6058351 Website: www.palermotourism.com

Located in the heart of Palermo's historic center, this tourist information point offers convenient access to maps, brochures, and guides, as well as assistance with transportation, accommodation, and sightseeing tours. Friendly staff are on hand to answer questions and provide helpful tips for exploring the city.

Tourist Information Office - Palermo Airport:
Address: Aeroporto Falcone e Borsellino, 90145 Cinisi PA, Italy Phone: +39 091 6058351 Website: www.palermotourism.com

Situated at Palermo's Falcone e Borsellino Airport, this information office provides essential services for travelers arriving in the city, including airport maps, transportation options, and tourist information. Staff can assist with hotel reservations, car rentals, and airport transfers, ensuring a smooth and stress-free arrival experience.

These tourist information centers are valuable resources for travelers seeking assistance and guidance during their stay in Palermo, offering a range of services and information to enhance their experience and ensure a memorable visit.

Emergency Contacts

In case of emergencies or urgent assistance, it's important to have access to the appropriate contacts and resources. Here are some essential emergency contacts for Palermo:

Police (Polizia di Stato): Emergency Number: 112 or 113

The Polizia di Stato is responsible for law enforcement and public safety in Palermo. In case of emergencies or criminal incidents, dial 112 to reach the police emergency hotline, where operators can dispatch officers and provide assistance as needed.

Medical Emergency (Ambulanza): Emergency Number: 118

In case of medical emergencies, including accidents, injuries, or sudden illnesses, dial 118 to request an ambulance. Trained medical personnel will respond to your location and provide emergency medical treatment or transport to the nearest hospital or medical facility.

Fire Department (Vigili del Fuoco): Emergency Number: 115

The Vigili del Fuoco is responsible for firefighting, rescue operations, and emergency response in Palermo. In case of fires, accidents, or other emergencies requiring assistance from the fire department, dial 115 to reach the emergency hotline and request immediate assistance.

Tourist Police (Polizia di Stato - Servizio Turistico): Phone: +39 091 743 4444

The Tourist Police unit specializes in assisting tourists and visitors to Palermo, providing information, assistance, and support in multiple languages. Contact the Tourist Police for non-emergency inquiries, lost property reports, or tourist-related assistance during your stay in the city.

Important Reminders:

If you are experiencing a life-threatening emergency, always call 112 immediately.

For non-emergencies, you can call the numbers listed above.

The Tourist Police can help you with a variety of issues, such as lost passports, stolen property, and directions.

By familiarizing yourself with these emergency contacts and resources, you can ensure that you're prepared to respond effectively in case of emergencies or unforeseen situations during your visit to Palermo. Stay informed, stay safe, and enjoy your time exploring this vibrant and enchanting city!

CONCLUSION

As we come to the end of this journey through the vibrant streets and rich history of Palermo, it's time to reflect on the experiences we've shared and the memories we've made along the way. From the majestic cathedrals and bustling markets to the hidden gems and cultural delights, Palermo has revealed itself as a city of endless wonders and timeless beauty.

Throughout this guide, we've explored the top attractions, cultural treasures, and culinary delights that define Palermo's unique charm and character. We've delved into its rich history, from ancient civilizations to medieval monarchs, and discovered the diverse influences that have shaped its cultural heritage over the centuries. We've savored the flavors of Sicilian cuisine, indulged in street food delights, and immersed ourselves in the vibrant art scene and colorful festivals that animate the city's streets.

But beyond the sights and sounds, Palermo has also offered us something deeper—a glimpse into the soul of Sicily, with its warmth, hospitality, and resilience in the face of adversity. We've met locals who have welcomed us with open arms, sharing their stories and traditions with pride and passion. We've forged connections with fellow travelers from around the world, united by our shared love of exploration and discovery.

As we bid farewell to Palermo, let us carry with us the lessons and memories we've gathered along the way. Let us remember the beauty of its sun-drenched piazzas, the fragrance of its citrus groves, and the laughter of its people echoing through the narrow alleys. Let us savor the taste of Sicilian cuisine on our tongues and the warmth of Sicilian hospitality in our hearts.

But let us also carry something more—a sense of curiosity, wonder, and appreciation for the world around us. Let us continue to seek out new adventures, explore unfamiliar cultures, and embrace the beauty of diversity in all its forms. Let us approach each day with open minds and open hearts, ready to learn, grow, and connect with the world and each other.

And let us remember that our journey doesn't end here—it's only just beginning. As we return home, may we carry the spirit of Palermo with us, inspiring us to live with passion, purpose, and joy. Let us share our stories, inspire others to embark on their own adventures, and spread the magic of travel wherever we go.

So, until we meet again, dear traveler, may your path be filled with wonder, your heart with joy, and your soul with the spirit of Palermo. Grazie mille e arrivederci, until we meet again in the eternal embrace of wanderlust and discovery. Buon viaggio!

Printed in Great Britain
by Amazon

44528965R00066